Admirable Americans-I

GROVER CLEVELAND
A Study in Political Courage

By

ROLAND HUGINS

WASHINGTON, D. C.

THE ANCHOR-LEE PUBLISHING COMPANY

1922

Printing Statement:

Due to the very old age and scarcity of this book,
many of the pages may be hard to read due to the
blurring of the original text, possible missing pages,
missing text, dark backgrounds and other issues
beyond our control.

Because this is such an important and rare work, we
believe it is best to reproduce this book regardless of
its original condition.

Thank you for your understanding.

A Foreword

Admirable Americans is a series of brief but complete biographies, dealing, for the most part, with leaders of the last generation who have died within recent memory. A tentative and partial list follows:

1. GROVER CLEVELAND
2. THEODORE ROOSEVELT
3. JOHN HAY
4. ANDREW D. WHITE
5. JOHN FISKE
6. "O. HENRY"
7. "MARK TWAIN"

Much of the biography which has appeared recently in America and in England has been written in a satirical or defamatory vein. The temper of the present series is quite different. Although these biographical sketches are intended to be just and impartial estimates, giving both the lights and shadows, the subjects themselves have been chosen for the reason that they are, on the whole, men worthy of esteem.

Surely it should not be necessary to apologize, in these days of studied mockery and supercilious ridicule, for the exercise of a little generous admiration. Says La Rochefoucauld: "To praise good actions heartily is in some measure to take part in them."

It is a mark of really first-rate men that the more we study them the greater grows our respect, liking and admiration. Grover Cleveland is one of the Americans who meets this test; he well repays a closer acquaintance.

Contents

Chronological Summary

EVENT	DATE	AGE
Born, Caldwell, N. J.	March 18, 1837	
Admitted to Bar	May, 1859	22
Took office as Mayor of Buffalo, N. Y.	January 1, 1882	45
Took office as Governor of New York State	January 1, 1883	46
Inaugurated as President of the United States	March 4, 1885	48
Married to Miss Frances Folsom	June 2, 1886	49
Defeated in Presidential Election	November, 1888	51
Inaugurated as President, Second Time	March 4, 1893	56
Died, Princeton, N. J.	June 24, 1908	71

GROVER CLEVELAND

I

LIFE AND CHARACTER

ROVER CLEVELAND left the White House at the end of his second occupancy, and retired to private life, in March, 1897. While a public leader is felt as contemporaneous, no one can be sure of his calibre. But in the retrospect across a quarter of a century it is possible to see a man justly. The controversies which quickened men's pulses a generation ago, before Bryan ever ran for President or the *Maine* sank, are now curiously cold. We are able today to read the lineaments of Cleveland's character without the distraction and distortion of partisanships.

Cleveland came rapidly to the fore once he had attracted the attention of the public. In the fall of 1881, at the age of forty-five, he was elected mayor of the city of Buffalo. Three years later he was elected President of the United States. In the decade that followed he was the leader and idol of the Democratic Party, and easily the dominant figure in the political life of the nation. The qualities in Cleveland which caught and held public esteem for him were these: moral courage and independence of spirit, painstaking industry, caution and thoroughness in the exploration of public questions, firmness in action after his mind was made up, and personal honesty raised almost to the pitch of a passion. People often spoke, in his time, of "Cleveland luck." It was a phrase misapplied. Roosevelt had luck—and made good use of it. But Cleveland's advancement, though rapid, was logical and orderly. He fought his way step by step. He had to fight both against the hostilities and rivalries which every public man encounters, and against his own limitations. He was intellectually able, but not brilliant. He developed the capacity to handle situations as they arose, but he did not make occasions. Although he never lost his hold on the respect of the country, there were times when his popularity and influence flickered low. When he stepped from power in 1897 he was under something of an eclipse. When he died, in 1908, he was everywhere recognized as a man who had not altogether missed greatness; and since his death his reputation and good repute have grown steadily.

On his father's side Cleveland was of English descent, on his mother's Irish and German. He was born at Caldwell, New Jersey, March 18, 1837, and christened Stephen Grover Cleveland. His father was a Presbyterian minister, who had received, at Yale, a college education: an advantage he was unable to give his sons. In 1841 his father accepted a pastorate at Fayetteville, New York, near Syracuse, at $600 a year. There were nine children. Grover, at the age of fourteen, left school for a year and worked in the village grocery store, thereby swelling the family income for that year by $50. When his father died in 1853, Grover followed his older brother, the Reverend William, to New York City, and worked under him, as clerk, at the New York Institution for the Blind. At the end of a year he returned home for a summer's vacation; sought work, unsuccessfully, in Utica and Syracuse; started for Cleveland, Ohio; stopped to visit his uncle in Buffalo; and there found employment and a home. He entered a law firm as helper and office boy. His pay, at first $4 a week, had in five years risen to the flattering sum of $50 a month. In that period he acquired a legal education, and was admitted to the bar in 1859, at the age of 22. He remained in the employ of the same firm, as law clerk, for four years more. In 1863 he was appointed assistant district attorney of Erie County.

Not a Soldier in Civil War

When the Civil War broke out, in 1861, Cleveland was 24 years old. To the calls for volunteers he did not respond. Two of his brothers served throughout the war, in the Union armies. Grover stayed with his law work. In 1863 he was drafted for service. In the Civil War a drafted man was permitted to furnish a substitute, or to pay for the procurement of a substitute. Cleveland paid $1,000, borrowing the money from his superior, the district attorney. This course afforded his political opponents, in later years, when he had become a candidate for high office, the opportunity to cry slacker. In 1892, for instance, during his second campaign against General Benjamin Harrison, Senator John Sherman of Ohio attacked his war record in the following language:

"There is this to be said of him, that he was a man full grown at the opening of the war, an able-bodied man when the war was on. I have never known, nor has it ever been proved, that he had any heart for or sympathies with the Union soldier or the Union cause."

In this there may have been a grain of truth. Cleveland chose to be a Democrat on attaining his majority, in 1858, when the War of Secession was brewing, and the alignments were being made. He undoubtedly followed the controversy closely, as did every other intelligent person; but his conclusions and convictions have not been recorded. During all of this period he was contributing heavily out of his earnings to the support of his widowed mother. His enlistment would have cancelled that help. We may at least be sure that he chose his course deliberately. And everything we know about his character leads us to believe that he was not a coward.

After a three years' grind as assistant district attorney, Cleveland ran for district attorney on the Democratic ticket, and was beaten. During the following fifteen years he devoted his attention to the practice of law, with the exception of a three years' interval, 1870-1873, when he was sheriff of Erie County, his first elective office. He was successively a member of the firms of Vanderpoel and Cleveland; Laning, Cleveland, and Folsóm; Bass, Cleveland and Bissel; and Cleveland, Bissel and Sicard. He gradually, in this period of a decade and a half, built a success and local reputation. He was known as a reliable and clear-headed lawyer, who took an interest in civic affairs, and who talked good sense; as a man who paid his bills on the nail and attended assiduously to his business: altogether a solid citizen. The Buffalo *Express*, a Republican newspaper, said of him editorially soon after his nomination for mayor in the autumn of 1881:

> "We know Grover Cleveland. Nearly all of his fellow-citizens are aware of his distinguished abilities and reputation as a lawyer, of his great personal worth, of his unswerving uprightness, and his high moral courage. But we know something more than all this. It has happened to us to have had personal experience of that sleepless vigilance, that tireless devotion, that singular penetration and that broad good judgment which Mr. Cleveland has always displayed in the interest of his clients, and from which so many have reaped the reward of a righteous verdict. If he is mayor, the city will be to him as his client—as a client standing more sorely in need of all his best endeavors than anyone he ever served before—and woe would be to the man that should attempt to rob or otherwise wrong her."

He accepted the nomination reluctantly. The Democrats put him forward because they believed they could win with him; and they did, rather easily. He was elected mayor by a majority of 3,530. Buffalo, to-day grown to be a city of over a half a million, had in 1881 a population of 160,000. It was the third city of New York State, and was typical of most American cities of the period in the shoddiness and venality of its politics. Municipal waste and corruption gave Cleveland his opportunity. The day he entered office he started to give the city a business administration. He discovered that the municipality was paying nearly twice as much as private persons for the construction of plank sidewalks; he found that the city auditor was performing his duties in a most perfunctory manner; he called attention to the fact that the municipal government was not getting a full working day from its employees. He pointed out that the city was paying far too much for street cleaning, for repairs to school buildings, and for public printing. He elaborated no general program of reform, seeking, rather, economy and efficiency in concrete instances.

A Plain-Spoken Mayor

Within a fortnight of his inauguration the Mayor vetoed an appropriation of the Common Council granting $800 to each of three German newspapers in payment for publishlishing a daily synopsis of the Council's proceedings. This was a hoary form of patronage. Cleveland declared that these subsidies were a sheer waste of public money, since the papers would in any event, as a matter of news, furnish their readers with some account of the proceedings of the Council. A few days later he vetoed a resolution directing the city clerk to draw a warrant for $500 in favor of the chairman of the Decoration Day Committee of the Grand Army of the Republic. He said that he was in sympathy with the object of the resolution—"the efforts of our veteran soldiers to keep alive the memory of their fallen comrades"—but insisted that the money for this purpose should be obtained through the voluntary subscriptions of citizens rather than through taxation. This act was characteristic of Cleveland. All through his career he refused to sanction the expenditure of public money merely because the object was deemed to be worthy. As Governor of New York he vetoed appropriations for soldiers' and sailors' monuments. As President he vetoed pension bills by the score. Only the stiffest kind of political courage will resist measures that are supposed to carry a patriotic appeal. Cleveland had that kind of courage.

One of Cleveland's messages to the Common Council became known as the "plain speech veto," and was widely quoted. The council had awarded the contracts for cleaning the paved streets and alleys of the city during the ensuing five year˞ to a favored bidder named Talbot, at a compensation of $422,500. The Mayor disapproved the resolution. He said:

"The bid accepted by your honorable body is more than one hundred thousand dollars higher than that of another responsible party for the same work; and a worse and more suspicious feature in this transaction is that the bid now accepted is fifty thousand dollars more than that made by Talbot himself within a very few weeks, openly and publicly to your honorable body, for performing precisely the same services. This latter circumstance is to my mind the manifestation on the part of the contractor of a reliance upon the forbearance and generosity of your honorable body, which would be more creditable if it were less expensive to the taxpayers.

"I am not aware that any excuse is offered for the acceptance of this proposal, thus increased, except that the lower bidders can not afford to do the work for the sums they name.

"This extreme tenderness and consideration for those who desire to contract with the city, and this touching and paternal solicitude lest they should be inprovidently led into a bad bargain, is, I am sure, an exception to general business rules, and seems to have no place in this selfish, sordid world, except as found in the administration of municipal affairs.

"The charter of your city requires that the Mayor, when he disapproves any resolution of your honorable body, shall return the same with his objections.

"This is a time for plain speech, and my objection to the action of your honorable body now under consideration shall be plainly stated. I withhold my assent from the same, because I regard it as the culmination of a most barefaced, impudent and shameless scheme to betray the interests of the people and to worse than squander the public money.

"I will not be misunderstood in this matter. There are those whose votes were given for this resolution whom I can not and will not suspect of a willful neglect of the interests they are sworn to protect; but it has been fully demonstrated that there are influences, both in and about your honorable body, which it behooves every honest man to watch and avoid with the greatest care."

By his "plain speech veto" Cleveland saved the city $109,000. A little later he effected a saving of $800,000, by pushing through, against the stubborn resistance of the Council, his plan for a special commission of five to supervise the construction of a new sewer system. The Common Council did not dare to override the vetoes of this blunt, outspoken, hard-hitting executive, for public opinion had aligned itself behind him. Before six months of his term of office had passed his methods and achievements had attracted attention in other parts of the State and nation.

The New York State Democratic Convention met that year in Syracuse. The delegates from western New York united to urge Cleveland as the nominee for governor. On the eve of the convention his supporters requested him, by telegraph, to come to Syracuse. He left Buffalo in the early evening, had a conference in Syracuse with Daniel Manning, party chieftain, and returned to Buffalo that same night. The next day he was nominated for governor on the third ballot. In the campaign which followed Cleveland attended to his duties as mayor. He did not make a single speech. His opponent on the Republican ticket was Charles J. Folger, Secretary of the Treasury under President Arthur. Cleveland's candidacy appealed especially to the independent voters. He was elected by a majority of 192,850.

In the two years that Cleveland occupied the Governor's chair at Albany he solidified his reputation for courage, honesty and common sense. On his recommendation the legislature (passed a State civil service law. He scrutinized expenditures; he cut off a useless Board of Canal Appraisers; disapproved a legislative deficiency bill; and vetoed a grant of $20,000 for the Catholic Protectory of New York City. He cancelled many appropriation items on the ground that they were gratuities—"purely donations." He said "my conception of public duty leads me to the conviction that the people pay taxes for their benefit and protection, and that forced contributions of the public funds are not justified except upon that theory."

The Governor's Vetoes

His veto messages were vigorous. The legislature passed a bill to "amend and consolidate the several acts relating to the city of Elmira." The Governor denounced it as "special legislation of the most objectionable character." The legislature put through a tenure of office bill applying especially to officials in New York City. Cleveland returned it with the comment: "Of all the defective and shabby legislation which has come before me, this is the worst and most inexcusable." A new charter for the city of Lyons he described as "a mass of impracticable inconsistencies and incongruous and useless crudities, which, if allowed to go upon our statute books, would be a disgrace to the State and the law-making power."

Among the scores of bills vetoed by Governor Cleveland were several granting special favors to corporations. He would not allow gas-light companies to use land without the owners' consent. He would not permit street car companies to monopolize municipal rights of way. He would not release the shareholders of banks and other corporations from the obligations they had assumed. These vetoes pleased the people. Cleveland could easily have posed as a champion of the people against the encroachment and greed of the corporations. But he was not posing. When a Five Cent Fare Bill, the result of popular clamor, was presented to him, he vetoed it promptly. At that time the elevated roads of New York City were charging different fares at different periods of the day. During three hours in the early morning and three in the late afternoon the fare was five cents; at all other times ten

cents. The bill which had passed the legis
lature proposed to make five cents the uni
form fare throughout the day. Clevelan
held public hearings on the measure. H
heard elaborate arguments from both sides
he studied the legal history of the question
and he decided that the proposal was unfai
In his veto message he said: "It seems t
me that to arbitrarily reduce these fares, a
this time and under existing circumstances
involves a breach of faith on the part of th
State." He explained his reasons for dissen
in a three thousand word argument. He ex
pected that his rejection of a measure spon
sored by workingmen, politicians and th
press would raise a storm against him. O
the contrary he found his message very wel
received. All the newspapers praised hin
for his temerity, and especially for the car
with which he had examined every aspect o
the subject. Cleveland never shirked th
labor necessary to make himself understood
He stated in full his reasons for his acts
The people like that trait in a man; a democ
racy appreciates the courtesy of explana
tions.

Among the questions which came to th
Governor's attention day by day were man
applications for pardon. Cleveland did no
delegate this task to subordinates, bu

probed personally each appeal for executive clemency, often reviewing the entire record of the cases before him. The newspapers charged that he was too lenient; that he was lavish in his pardons and commutations of sentence. In an interview Cleveland answered these criticisms:

> "The pardoning power is one of the most difficult and perplexing duties that a Governor has to perform. * * * Occasionally there is an epidemic of a particular class of crime in a section of the State; the public becomes excited, and it sometimes occurs that a man is convicted on insufficient evidence at a time when public sentiment is high; he receives a long sentence and, perhaps, all contrary to facts."

It was Cleveland's habit to get at the facts.

While Governor, Cleveland made few speeches. In his two annual messages to the legislature he confined himself to State issues, with the exception of a single passage on the decline of the American merchant marine, in the course of which he quoted de Tocqueville. Widespread interest had by this time been aroused in this burly, independent figure, who took orders from nobody, and declined to cater to politicians, or men of wealth, or representatives of labor.

His availability as a Presidential candidate was emphasized by the fact that he had proved his strength in New York State. During the quarter century which followed the Civil War national elections were close, and popular majorities small. To capture the electoral vote of the larger States was, therefore, the primary concern of party managers.

A Campaign of Personalities

The Democratic national convention which met at Chicago in July, 1884, nominated Cleveland on the second ballot. The Chairman of the Convention said of Cleveland's admirers: "They love him and they respect him, not only for himself, for his integrity and judgment and iron will, but they love him most of all for the enemies he has made." During the campaign Cleveland spoke but twice. His Republican opponent, the brilliant and magnetic James G. Blaine, of Maine, stumped the country from end to end. The debate was supposed to center about the tariff; it actually consisted, in large part, of bitter personalities and of appeals to partisan prejudice. Blaine argued that to entrust the Democrats with power would be "to call to the administration of the government the men who organized the

Rebellion." A Democratic victory, he asserted, "would rekindle smouldering passions." This was familiar ground to Blaine. For years he had been active in the politics of Reconstruction, and had been one of the most adroit of those politicians who made capital out of the memories of the Civil War: a game then known as "waving the bloody shirt." Cleveland, on the other hand, represented a newer school and a different interest, which looked chiefly to a reform of political and economic evils.

In this campaign of 1884 floods of personal abuse were loosed. In some recent Presidential contests candidates have been made the victims of whispering campaigns, by which slanders have been spread as gossip. In those earlier days the mud was spread openly in the newspapers, and thrown by the spellbinders. The Mulligan letters, which had come to light eight years previously during a Congressional investigation of Blaine's conduct as Speaker of the House, were reprinted and scattered broadcast. These letters indicated that Blaine had used his official position to obtain bonds and large loans from the Union Pacific, the Northern Pacific, and the Little Rock and Fort Smith Railroads. Although the "Plumed Knight" had defended himself with skill, he had failed to convince the more fastidious that he embodied the soul of honor. Many scurrilous stories about Cleveland were circulated. No one impugned his pecuniary probity; but it was charged that his habits were coarse and his tastes vulgar; that he consorted with low companions; that he frequently had been picked up drunk on the streets of Buffalo and carried home; that he was a habitual gambler; and that he courted the society of dissolute women. One highly embroidered and scandalous tale elicited from Cleveland the comment: "Tell the truth!" This message was the only reply that he deigned to make to any of the slanderers. All of the charges were gross exaggerations. Some of them sounded plausible because they were spun around a small core of fact. Cleveland was distinctly of the type known as a man's man. He was not a hypocrite; and he was not a Puritan. All his life he drank to some extent; and he played poker occasionally. These were his chief sins. But the calumnies clung to him for many years.

Late in the campaign Cleveland was asked to sanction the release of a yarn concerning an early indiscretion of his opponent, but he spurned the suggestion. Some of his supporters were less scrupulous; and the story

was published. Blaine was beaten, in the
end, quite as much by dissension in the Republican ranks as by the exertions of the
Democrats. He was repudiated by a group
of Republican independents, including
Henry Ward Beecher, William Everett, Carl
Schurz, and George William Curtis. The independents became known as "Mugwumps."
Six days before the campaign closed the Rev.
Dr. Samuel Burchard, one of a delegation of
clergyman who waited on Blaine in New
York City, made the following pledge of
loyalty: "We are Republicans, and we do
not propose to leave our party and identify
ourselves with the party of Rum, Romanism,
and Rebellion!" Blaine heard; but he did
not grasp the damaging significance of the
words. They alienated some of his Catholic
supporters in a State where, as the returns
showed, every vote counted.

First Term as President

The result in the Empire State was in
doubt for several days. In the rest of the
country the Republicans had secured 182 of
the electoral votes, and the Democrats 183.
On the swing New York's 36 electoral votes,
therefore, hinged the election. As soon as it
was apparent that the contest would be close,
the Democratic State Committee sent tele-

grams to all local headquarters, instructing them to detail vigorous and courageous men to watch the count. Cleveland made an announcement which was bulletined throughout the country: "I believe I have been elected President, and nothing but the grossest fraud can keep me out of it, and that we will not permit." After several days of tension the official tabulations showed that Cleveland had carried New York State by 1,149 votes. His popular majority in the country at large was 62,680. Shortly after the New Year he sent to the State legislature his last message, remarkable for its brevity. It read:

"To THE LEGISLATURE:
"I hereby resign the office of Governor of the State of New York."

Grover Cleveland was the first Democrat to occupy the White House in twenty-four years. He came into office with a horde of hungry partisans pressing at his back. Practically all the Federal offices were held by Republicans; and he was urged to make a clean sweep. In fact, he was never given a minute's rest by the place hunters. In principle the President was a believer in Civil Service reform. Professional office seekers he held in contempt. He resisted the pressure put upon him; and when he yielded he did so reluctantly and late, with the result that the embittered politicians publicly scolded him. On the other hand Civil Service reformers were equally displeased. They pointed out that in two years Cleveland changed 40,000 fourth-class postmasters in a total of 52,600; 2,000 Presidential postmasters in 2,380; 100 collectors of customs in 111; 84 internal revenue collectors in 85; 65 district attorneys in 70; and 32 foreign ministers in 33. To make the circle of dissatisfaction complete, the President himself was irritated and aggrieved. In speaking of this period he afterward said to an associate: "You know the things in which I yielded; but no one save myself can ever know the things which I resisted." At another time he wrote: "I doubt if I shall advise any one to lose the support of party in the hope of finding support among those who beyond partizanship profess a patriotic desire for good government." Cleveland's attitude on patronage boiled down to this: that he had, in nine cases out of ten, little reluctance in replacing a Republican with a Democrat, but he strongly preferred a competent Democrat to a party hack. Such a practice was better than a return to the spoils system. It appeared to elicit, however, a maximum of criticism.

On one subject Cleveland found occasion to lecture Congress in the same sarcastic tone that he used at Buffalo and Albany. A stream of private pension bills came to his desk for signature. He vetoed about one in seven: three hundred vetoes in all. In his veto messages he made it apparent that either the claimants were swindlers, or that their contentions were ill-founded. Furthermore he vetoed the "dependent pension bill," which proposed to give to every honorably discharged veteran of the Civil War a pension of twelve dollars monthly. By this obduracy on pensions he incurred the enmity of the Grand Army of the Republic. This organization, founded in 1868, had by 1888 a membership of 400,000, and was supposed to control a million votes. The ex-soldiers accused Cleveland of being an enemy of the veterans, and a tool of "rebel brigadiers." In May, 1887, the President ordered that the flags in the custody of the War Department, both Union and Confederate, should be returned to the respective States. This "rebel flag order" was violently denounced throughout the North and West. The President had, indeed, exceeded his authority in issuing such an order, and he was obliged to rescind it. In 1905, eighteen years later, Congress authorized the return of the flags to the States.

In foreign affairs the President was firm and forehanded, although no momentous international question came to the fore during his first term. He suppressed, with United States marines, a revolt on the Isthmus of Panama. He sent a man-of-war to Ecuador to obtain the release of an American citizen. He negotiated a treaty with Great Britain which, had it been concluded, would have ended the long-standing dispute over the Canadian fisheries; but the Senate refused to ratify the agreement. He rebuked the Austrian government for refusing to receive an American minister on the ground that his wife was a Jewess. He sent Sackville-West, the British minister, home for an indiscretion in the campaign of 1888.

Wedded in the White House

Like James Buchanan, Grover Cleveland was a bachelor when elected President. His sister, Miss Rose Cleveland, directed the domestic and social activities of the White House during the first year of his incumbency. On June 2, 1886, in the Blue Room of the White House, he was married to Miss Frances Folsom, the daughter of a former law partner in Buffalo. Mrs. Cleveland was twenty-two years old: a tall, graceful, dignified girl, with a winning and tactful manner, who, as mistress of the Executive Mansion, won a wide popularity. Their first child, Ruth, who became known throughout the country as "Baby Cleveland," was born in 1891.

As his term wore on Cleveland's policies took more definite shape. He revoked, through the Land Office, many grants of the public domain unlawfully obtained by railroads and speculators, and restored over 100,000,000 acres to the use of homesteaders. He did what he could, after two decades of jobbery in the Navy Department, to create the nucleus of a modern fleet. He gradually became convinced that the Bland-Allison Act of 1878, under which the government was compelled, each month, to coin not less than $2,000,000 nor more than $4,000,000 in silver dollars, would eventually drain the Treasury of gold, and he recommended its repeal. The more he studied the tariff the more certain he grew that the high protective duties then in force were responsible for two evils: first, they built up a large surplus of revenue and invited extravagant appropriations —always to him anathema; and second, they imposed, both directly and indirectly, unnecessary burdens on the consumer. Although loath to admit it, he tended strongly toward the orthodox doctrines of free trade.

His annual message of 1887 was an innovation. He devoted every line of it to a discussion of the tariff. He attacked high protection with hammer and tongs, using both theoretical and practical arguments. The friends to whom he showed the message in advance strongly advised him to reconsider, declaring it would lose the next election. He replied: "It is more important to the country that this message should be delivered to Congress and the people than that I should be reelected President." Cleveland came to his conclusions slowly, by processes of investigation and reasoning, and when once he thought he had mastered a subject, and felt that he had the right of it, he never let go. A year later he told the Speaker of the House, "I want to tell you now that if every other man in the country abandons this issue I shall stick to it." A tariff bill sponsored by the administration was introduced in Congress, but failed of passage. Although the House of Representatives was Democratic during these four years, the Senate remained Republican, by a small majority.

Cleveland was renominated by the Democratic national convention which met at St.

Louis in 1888, by acclamation. The Republicans nominated General Benjamin Harrison, an Indiana lawyer, a Civil War hero, and the grandson of President William Henry Harrison. The campaign was comparatively quiet. A truce was called on personalities. Although the President received a popular majority of 98,000 in the country at large, he lost the larger States by narrow margins. The electoral vote stood 233 to 168 in Harrison's favor.

Cleveland took up residence in New York City, and resumed the practice of law. He had accumulated, by his savings and by judicious investments in real estate, about $75,000. During the next four years he did not devote himself entirely to legal work. He was in great demand as a speaker. Invitations poured in asking him to address all sorts of public gatherings. When he accepted, he carefully prepared his speech. He addressed audiences in New England, New York, Pennsylvania, Ohio, and Michigan, choosing as subjects topics of current interest—ballot reform, tariff problems, the monetary standard, and political ideals. He made about ten speeches a year: forty altogether in this period. He also carried on an extensive correspondence. In February, 1891, he was asked by the Reform Club of New York to express his opinion of the free coinage of silver. This was a time when nearly all politicians, in view of the great agitation in the West, were trying to prove themselves, in some fashion or other, the "friends of silver." Cleveland did not equivocate; he gave utterance to his convictions. In his letter he declared against "the dangerous and reckless experiment of free, unlimited, and independent silver coinage." The next morning his letter appeared in every newspaper. Like most seemingly rash acts of political courage it evoked more praise than criticism.

As the Presidential contest of 1892 drew near, the rank and file of the Democratic party turned to Cleveland. Some of the politicians, however, were of a different mind. David B. Hill of New York summoned a State convention to meet on February 22, fully three months before the usual time. This "snap convention" pledged the New York delegation to Hill; but the trick proved to be a boomerang. The New York friends of Cleveland organized as "Anti-Snappers," and called a convention of their own. In the rest of the country the tide for Cleveland was irresistible. When the national Democratic convention met at Chicago in June, more than two-thirds of the delegates voted for Cleveland on the first ballot. The Republicans had renominated President Harrison.

A Period of Popularity

This campaign of 1892 turned on the tariff. Early in Harrison's administration the Republicans had passed the McKinley Bill, a very tall protective measure. Prices of commodities rose immediately. As a consequence the Republicans were badly mauled in the Congressional elections of 1890. McKinley himself lost his seat. This unpopular schedule was still in force in 1892, and received the concentrated fire of the Democrats. When the votes were counted Cleveland's popular majority was found to be 380,000, the highest he had ever received. The electoral vote was: Cleveland 277, Harrison 145.

The election of 1892 was a personal triumph for Grover Cleveland; in popularity it marked the peak of his career. He came to the Presidency the second time at the age of 56, in the full maturity of his powers. Long administrative experience and the weight of great responsibility had broadened an intelligence that was always robust, and made adamant a will that had never yielded to expediency. In the following four years he had need of every ounce of his strength. He was forced to break his way through a jungle of difficulties. He had need, indeed, for qualities that he did not possess, for great powers of conciliation, persuasion and tolerance. He met every issue firmly: silver surplus, tariff revision, bond issues, the Pullman railroad strike, the Venezuelan boundary dispute. In each encounter he fought through to some sort of a finish; but in each crisis he roused a bitter opposition. He successively alienated nearly every large section of public opinion. When he left the White House in 1897, he went out under a pall of disapproval, although like all men who look primarily to their consciences for approval, he was unperturbed.

During his second term Cleveland played an independent hand in regard to appointments. He flatly refused to place his time at the mercy of office-seekers. He issued an Executive Order which made Washington gasp:

"The time which was set apart for the reception of Senators and Representatives has been almost entirely spent in listening to applications for office, which have been bewildering in volume, perplexing and exhausting in their iterations, and impossible of remembrance.

"A due regard for public duty obliges

me to decline, from and after this date, all personal interviews with those seeking appointments to office, except as I on my own motion may especially invite them. Applicants for office will only prejudice their prospects by repeated importunity and by remaining in Washington·to await results."

For many months previous to the inauguration in March, 1893, business conditions had been unsound. In June banks began to fail, and factories to close. By July a panic was in full swing. On June 30, the President issued a proclamation summoning an extra session of Congress to meet August 7. In his special message of August 8 he attributed the financial and commercial distress of the country mainly to the operations of the Sherman silver purchase act of July 14, 1890. This statute, which had superseded the Bland-Allison Act, required the Government to purchase, each month, 4,500,-000 ounces of silver, and to issue against this bullion, up to its full value, legal tender notes redeemable on demand in coin. Since the holder of the notes was permitted under a Treasury ruling to exercise his option, these coin certificates were really payable in gold. Between July, 1890, and July, 1893, the gold coin and bullion in the

Treasury had fallen off by $132,000,000, while silver coin and bullion had increased by $147,000,000. The President demanded immediate action. In the House a bill to repeal the silver purchase act was introduced August 11, and passed August 28. But in the Senate the advocates of silver attempted to talk the bill to death. During the course of the filibuster one sitting lasted three nights and days. After two months of obstruction Cleveland managed to jam the measure through, 48 to 37. But in the process he depleted his powers of Senatorial coercion.

When Congress reconvened for its regular session in December, the President declared that:

> "After a hard struggle, tariff reform is directly before us. Nothing so important claims our attention, and nothing so clearly presents itself as both an opportunity and a duty. After full discussion, our countrymen have spoken in favor of this reform, and they have confided the work of its accomplishment to the hands of those who are solemnly pledged to it."

Representative William Wilson introduced a tariff bill which embodied the President's ideas. It provided for free wool, copper, coal, iron ore, lumber and sugar; and made moderate reductions in the duties on consumption articles. In the House the bill fared well, passing by a vote of 182 to 106. But in the Senate it was twisted and mutilated. Everything but wool and copper was removed from the free list. In all, the Senate made 634 changes in the House bill. Even this patchwork measure was passed, after a four months' delay, with difficulty, by a vote of 39 to 34. The President was infuriated. In a letter to Congressman Wilson he protested: "Every true Democrat knows that this bill in the present form is not the consummation for which we have long looked. Our abandonment of the cause or the principles upon which it rests means perfidity and party dishonor." But the Senate would not recede an inch, and the House was forced to accept the Senate amendments in their entirety. Although Cleveland would not put his name to the measure, he did not care to veto it, since it made an average reduction of eleven per cent in the duties of the McKinley tariff, and since, furthermore, it composed the only kind of tariff legislation that he could get. He allowed it to become a law without his signature. He gave voice, however, to his disgust:

"Tariff reform will not be settled until it is honestly and fairly settled, in

the interest and to the benefit of a
patient and long-suffering people. I
take my place with the rank and file of
the Democratic party, who are not
blinded to the fact that the livery of the
Democratic tariff reform has been
stolen and worn in the service of Republican protection."

Dwindling Gold Reserves

The President had hoped that the repeal
of the Sherman Silver Purchase Act and the
enactment of a new tariff law would dispel
the industrial depression from which the
country was suffering, and relieve the Treasury of its embarrassments. But he soon en-
countered even worse difficulties. There were
outstanding at this time about $346,000,000
in greenbacks, behind which stood a gold
fund of $100,000,000, while other issues of
paper currency brought the total of notes in
circulation to approximately $500,000,000
The silver certificates, issued under the
Bland-Allison Act of 1878, were redeemable
in silver. The coin notes, issued under the
Sherman Act of 1890, were redeemable in
coin, that is, in either gold or silver, at the
option of the Treasury. Cleveland decided
that all of the Government paper, greenbacks, silver certificates, and coin notes,
should, in fair financial weather or foul, be

redeemed in gold. Any other course, he thought, would cast a doubt on "the good faith and honest intentions of the Government's professions, or create a suspicion of our country's solvency." Such a policy contained grave dangers. By law the currency was inelastic; and in practice gold was drawn from the Treasury not alone by the timid, but chiefly by those whose only purpose was profit. In this situation the President unquestionably could have checked the raid on gold by putting into circulation a portion of the Treasuy's stock of silver. But he had ruled otherwise, and having made his decision he sustained it with inflexible determination. As a consequence he was forced to sell government bonds in a period of peace, for the first time in the country's history.

In April, 1893, the Treasury's gold redemption fund fell below $100,000,000. By January 1, 1894, it was down to $70,000,000. On January 17, the President directed that an issue of $50,000,000 in United States bonds be offered for sale in exchange for gold. By this method the gold reserve was built up to $107,000,000. But by November of the same year the fund had dwindled to $61,000,000. A second issue of $50,000,000 in bonds was offered for gold. This issue was taken up by a syndicate of thirty-three banking-houses. The banks, holding their own gold out of the public's reach, were finding it profitable to siphon gold from the Treasury and sell it back for bonds. Three months after the second bond sale, in February, 1895, there remained only $41,000,-000 in the government's gold reserve. In this emergency the President appealed to J. Pierpont Morgan and other financiers in New York. An arrangement was reached whereby a banking syndicate agreed to pay $65,117,000 in gold for $62,515,000 in 4 per cent bonds. The bankers also pledged themselves to "exert all financial influence and make all legitimate efforts to protect the Treasury of the United States against the withdrawal of gold." After this the drive on the Treasury ceased. The 4 per cent bonds, however, which had been obtained from the government at 104½, were offered for sale on the open market, and immediately went to 118, giving the bankers and financiers a profit on the transaction of $7,-000,000. Criticism of the President's Treasury policy, which had been constant and bitter, now rose, in some quarters, to a pitch of frenzy.

Debs and the Pullman Strike

In the meantime, labor disturbances had broken out, for the panic of 1893 was followed by industrial stagnation. Throngs of the unemployed, augmented by vagabonds and tramps, roamed about the country. "Coxey's army" straggled into Washington. There were strikes and lockouts in many industries. In May, 1894, the Pullman Palace Car Company dismissed a part of its workmen, and reduced the wages of the remainder. The men struck, and submitted a request for arbitration, to which the Company replied, "We have nothing to arbitrate." The cause of the Pullman employees was taken up by the American Railway Union, an organization of about 150,000 railroad workers, with headquarters in Chicago. The president of the union was Eugene V. Debs, then a young man. A general railroad strike was called for June 26, and after that day switchmen refused to attach Pullman cars to any train, while engineers and crews refused to move any train in which Pullman cars were included. Within five days practically every road running out of Chicago was tied up. The strike spread as far as the Pacific States, and passenger and mail trains to which Pullman cars were attached could not be moved.

At this juncture the Federal government intervened. Attorney-General Olney (afterward made Secretary of State) directed United States counsel in Chicago to apply to the Federal courts for an injunction. The next day, July 1, Judge Woods issued a sweeping injunction forbidding Debs and the other officers of the Railway Union from interfering with the transportation of the mails and from obstructing interstate commerce, and also forbidding them from attempting to persuade railroad employees to strike. There had been sporadic outbreaks of violence in the Chicago yards on June 30. The injunction aroused angry passions, and violence became general: cars were smashed and trains ditched. A marshal who read the injunction to the mob was hooted. On July 3, the President ordered Federal troops to move into Chicago. Governor Altgeld of Illinois protested in two long telegrams against the use of Federal Troops, but President Cleveland curtly refused to heed his objections. On July 7 the troops were given orders to shoot to kill. In clashes between the soldiers and the strikers during the next few days, members of the mob were killed. Violence ceased, and trains began to move. Debs and three of his associates were arrested, July 17, on a charge of contempt of court. They refused to give bail. On December 14, Debs was sentenced to six months in prison, and each of his associates to three months, on the charge of contempt.

The action of the Federal government in this strike provoked, especially in labor circles, a great deal of hostile comment. Many of the criticisms, however, missed the point. The President was well within his constitutional and legal rights in using the United States army to move the mails. Where the administration laid itself open to blame was in the abuse of the power of the Federal courts. It employed "government by injunction," not merely to protect the mails and to suppress violence, but to break a strike without reference to the merits of the dispute. The President later appointed a Commission, the members of which were Carrol D. Wright, John D. Kernan and Nicholas E. Worthington, to investigate the origin of the strike. In its report the Commission found less to censure in the conduct of the Railway Union than in the acts of its opponent, the Railway Managers' Association.

The Venezuelan Crisis

Only one action of Cleveland in his second term was greeted with general approval. That was his Venezuelan message. For

more than half a century Great Britain and
Venezuela had been disputing over the
boundary line of the colony of British Guiana. As early as 1876 Venezuela had appealed to the government of the United
States to interest itself in the matter. The
question was historical and geographical,
and a proper subject for the consideration of
impartial experts. The South American republic had pressed for arbitration, but Great
Britain had adopted a policy of postponement and delay. In the seventies rich deposits of gold were discovered in the areas
under dispute. These discoveries strengthened the disinclination of Great Britain to
submit the issue to arbitration, and furthermore seemed to convince her that her previous claims had been much too moderate.
She put forth a series of new demands,
which, had they been sustained, would have
added several substantial strips of territory
to her colony. In 1887 Venezuela had withdrawn its minister from London. The
United States, thereafter, several times suggested to Great Britain that the boundary
dispute be arbitrated, but without avail.
Cleveland decided to bring the matter to a
head. He feared not only an encroachment
on Venezuela, but a violation of the Monroe
Doctrine. In July, 1894, the Department of

State addressed a despatch to the British Foreign Office, once more urging arbitration. To this Lord Salisbury replied that "Her Majesty's Government could not consent to any departure from the Schomburgk line." The next American note was firmer in tone. Secretary of State Olney declared that the United States is "entitled to resent and resist any sequestration of Venezuelan soil by Great Britain." Salisbury waved this aside, with the remark that the Monroe Doctrine had "no foundation in the law of nations." Thereupon Cleveland sent to Congress his special message of December 17, 1895, which carried a hint of war. The President asserted that it was incumbent upon the United States to determine, "with sufficient certainty for its justification, what is the true divisional line" between Venezuela and British Guiana. To this end he requested Congress to make—

> "an adequate appropriation for the expenses of a Commission to be appointed by the Executive, who shall make the necessary investigations, and report upon the matter with the least possible delay. When such a report is made and accepted, it will, in my opinion, be the duty of the United States to resist, by every means in its power, as a wilful aggression upon its rights and interests,

the appropriation by Great Britain of any lands, or the exercise of governmental jurisdiction over any territory which, after investigation, we have determined of right belongs to Venezuela. In making these recommendations, I am fully alive to the responsibility incurred, and keenly realize all the consequences which may follow."

In Congress this message was greeted with wild applause. An appropriation of $100,000 for the expenses of the boundary commission was passed at once. Throughout the country the President's bold stand brought an enthusiastic response. William McKinley, then Governor of Ohio, and beginning to bulk large as a Presidential possibility, telegraphed: "The message is American in letter and spirit; and, in a calm, dispassionate manner, upholds the honor of the nation and ensures its security." Only in certain academic and financial circles on the Eastern seaboard was the message viewed with displeasure. On the New York Stock Exchange there was a drop of $400,-000,000 in the value of American securities. But war did not come. After a period of cogitation the British government decided to submit the matter to arbitration, Schomburgk line and all. A final award was rendered, in 1899, by an international commission sitting in Paris. The decision was in the nature of a compromise, and was regarded as being, on the whole, not unfavorable to Great Britain.

Retirement Under Fire

Notwithstanding Cleveland's promptness to resist anything that looked like aggression, his foreign policy in general might be termed anti-imperialistic. At the very beginning of his second term he withdrew from the Senate a treaty for the annexation of Hawaii, because he believed that the revolt in the Islands had been engineered with the secret connivance of American officials; and for four years he held the annexationists at bay. Furthermore, he did what he could to stave off a war with Spain. He offered friendly mediation from time to time. Otherwise he maintained a strict neutrality. He enforced the laws against filibustering expeditions so rigidly that he incurred the hostility of American sympathizers with the Cuban insurrectionists. However, in his final message to Congress, transmitted in December, 1896, after General Weyler's concentration order had been issued, he read Spain a plain warning. He said:

"The United States is not a nation to which peace is a necessity. * * *

When the inability of Spain to deal successfully with the insurrection has become manifest and it is demonstrated that her sovereignty is extinct in Cuba for all purposes of its rightful existence, and when a hopeless struggle for its reestablishment has degenerated into a strife which means nothing more than the useless sacrifice of human life and the utter destruction of the very subject-matter of the conflict, a situation will be presented in which our obligations to the sovereignty of Spain will be superseded by higher obligations, which we can hardly hesitate to recognize and discharge."

As Cleveland approached the end of his Presidential career he found himself the object of much ill-will. The South, the West, the North, had turned against him. The Congressional elections of 1894 had gone Republican by large majorities; and the Republicans were jubilant over their prospects for 1896. The Democratic Party had been captured by the advocates of free silver. Cleveland endeavored to rally the supporters of "honest money" within the Democratic ranks. "A cause worth fighting for," he said, "is worth fighting for to the end." But his efforts were futile. At the Democratic national convention which met at Chicago in June, 1896, Cleveland's name was not cheered, and his administration was not endorsed. Cleveland afterwards said: "Any man with even the smallest knowledge of the conditions which surrounded my second administration knows that I could not have commanded the support of half a dozen delegates in the whole country. The persistent misrepresentations of personal enemies, the falsehood and partisan denunciations published in the Republican press, betrayal by the advocates of free silver, and resistance to the declaration of war with Spain, had combined to make my administration one of the most unpopular in our history." There were other causes for discontent: the bond sales, the use of the Federal injunction against labor, low wages and unemployment. The man's great services were forgotten, and he was blamed for everything and anything. The Democrats nominated Bryan; and the Republicans swept triumphantly into office behind McKinley on a platform of high protectionism and gold monometalism.

On March 5, 1897, Cleveland retired finally from public life, and went to live in Princeton, New Jersey. He was made a trustee of Princeton University. He made occasional speeches to the undergraduates, and for a time delivered two lectures a year. There he wrote two books, "Presidential

Problems," and "Fishing and Shooting Sketches." He consistently refused, however, to prepare an autobiography. He abstained from participation in public affairs, except to give his endorsement, from time to time, to the conservative wing of the Democratic party. In 1905 he became one of a board of three trustees to administer the majority of the stock of the Equitable Life Assurance Company of New York. He did much to restore the confidence of the public, shaken by revelations of gross mismanagement, in the great insurance companies. He was engaged in this work at the time he was stricken with his last illness. He died at his home in Princeton, June 24, 1908, at the age of 71. The funeral, in conformity with his wishes, was simple, and was attended only by relatives and intimate friends. President Roosevelt, in announcing his death to the country, said: "The nation has been deprived of one of its greatest citizens."

Personal Characteristics

In physical appearance Cleveland belonged to the plain, hearty, dependable-looking type. In a large head were set blue eyes, strong nose and jaw, and a firm mouth. He was a heavy man; most of his life he was corpulent. His height was an inch or two under six feet. In Buffalo and Albany he had a stolid look, and something of a slouch. As he grew older his bearing took on more dignity, and his face more force. In his elder years he looked seamed and rugged.

His health and digestion were excellent. He had no nerves; there was not a hint of the neurotic about him. In 1893 a serious operation was secretly performed on the roof of his mouth, while he was aboard the yacht of his friend Commodore E. C. Benedict, in New York harbor. He stood the strain so well and recuperated so rapidly that no one outside of a small circle of intimates suspected the President's condition. A prodigious worker, he was also an ardent sportsman. He was particularly fond of fishing and of duck-hunting. While President he often went up the Potomac for bass or down the Bay for bluefish. He arranged his vacations so he could be out-of-doors most of the time: in the Adirondacks, in the Southern uplands, or on the coast. In the interim between his first and second terms as President he purchased a house, "Gray Gables," at Buzzard's Bay, Massachusetts, where he found the fishing good. This was thereafter his summer home.

Cleveland's manner usually was reserved and quiet; sometimes it verged on shyness.

He eschewed all affectations. He was ordinarily simple and cordial, but he did not coddle people. He was a good listener, and when he was not sympathetic with his caller's views he listened to the point of painfulness, letting the other man do all the talking. He could be frigid on occasion. He once told a young man who insisted on having his opinion: "That, sir, is a matter of too great importance to discuss in a five-minute interview, now rapidly drawing to its close." If he ever found that a man had lied to him, he never trusted that man again. In a conference with Boss Croker of Tammany Hall he lost his temper and pounded the table. And this was not the only time in his life when he spoke his views with energy. However, he was not addicted to profanity or slang; and there was a touch of quality in all he said.

With children he was kindly and friendly; he had a soft place in his heart for all little ones. He was happy in his home circle. Many episodes in his life betray a graceful courtesy. One of his first acts when he became President in 1885 was to restore the impoverished Grant to full rank and pay as general. On the last day that he was President, in 1897, he had a long, amicable conversation with McKinley on pending problems. He wished the incoming Republican President a successful administration, and expressed the hope that when he left the White House he would not be so glad as his predecessor to lay down the burden.

Cleveland never went abroad; apparently he had little desire to see the world. His only excursion outside the United States was a trip to Bermuda when a lawyer in Buffalo. Likewise there were certain mental frontiers that his mind seldom crossed. He had scant curiosity about literature, music or art. His reading was confined largely to American history and biography. He has left us no great orations, and also no cheap declamations, although he had opportunities: the unveiling of the Statue of Liberty, the opening of the Brooklyn Bridge, the funeral of General Grant. Many of his state papers are still readable. His fondness for heavy platitude would have been irksome had it not been relieved often by a sly play of humor. The care that he took to master a subject is evidenced in the cogency of his reasoning. Whatever the limitations of his mind, he at least possessed that one quality which is the surest guide to truth: intellectual integrity. He was willing to follow wherever the facts seemed to lead. He wrote everything carefully, making numerous drafts and revisions. His style tended at times to be elaborate and turgid, but it was seldom without flashes of vigor.

Some of Cleveland's phrases were long remembered and widely quoted, especially: "innocuous desuetude," "offensive partisans," "pernicious activity," and "the restless rich." When candidate for mayor in Buffalo, Cleveland said: "Public officials are the trustees of the people." This was one of the many echoes of Henry Clay's declaration, made in 1829: "Government is a trust, and the officers of the government are trustees; and both the trust and the trustees are created for the benefit of the people." In a shorter form,—"Public office is a public trust,"—this sentiment was long employed as a slogan by Cleveland's campaign managers. It did good service, because it applied.

Some of the more pungent of Cleveland's sentences were these:

"Party honesty is party expediency."

"It is a condition which confronts us, not a theory."

"Though the people support the government, the government should not support the people."

Political Philosophy

Everyone, it is safe to say, has some sort of a social philosophy, some theory of the state, some ideal of political and economic justice. Most of us, of course, accept the beliefs and assumptions which are current in our country and in our age, as natural and sound. And so it was with Cleveland; his social and economic philosophy was to some extent conventional, and to some extent unformulated. His was not a speculative turn of mind. He was the opposite of the doctrinnaire; certainly he had no general schemes for the remaking of society. Many of his acts and utterances seemed to show a strong bias toward conservatism; for example, his stand in the Pullman strike. When Governor of New York he found occasion to remark: "It is manifestly important that invested capital should be protected." On the other hand he often called vested interests sharply to account. In one of his messages to Congress (December 3, 1888), he wrote:

"Communism is a hateful thing and a menace to peace and organized government; but the communism of combined wealth and capital, the outgrowth of overweening cupidity and selfishness, which insidiously undermine the justice and integrity of free institutions, is not less dangerous than the communism of oppressed poverty and toil, which, exasperated by injustice and discontent, attacks with wild disorder the citadel of rule."

To attempt to label this man of action as one thing or another in the terms of political abstraction, is quite to miss the point. His doctrine was essentially individual and moral, and the direct outgrowth of his temperament and character. He himself was honest and downright in private business, and equally honest and downright in public affairs. His rule for statesmanship can, in its elements, be found in the two following quotations:

> "There is surely no difference in his duties and obligations, whether a person is entrusted with the money of one man or many; and yet it sometimes appears as though the office holder assumes that a different rule of fidelity prevails between him and the taxpayers than that which should regulate his conduct, when, as an individual, he holds the money of his neighbors."

And again:

> "An absolute and undivided responsibility on the part of the appointing power accords with correct business principles, the application of which to public affairs will always, I believe, direct the way to good administration and the protection of the people's interests."

To preach and moralize is ever easy; and nearly all public men are dripping with lofty sentiments. Cleveland distinguished himself by meaning what he said. To every office he gave the best that was in him: a thorough, painstaking, scrupulous administration. He did what he could, further, to balk and thwart the designs of selfish and greedy politicians. He could say "No" often, finally, and convincingly. His twenty-one predecessors in the Presidential chair sent to Congress, altogether, about one hundred and fifty vetoes. During his first term alone Cleveland sent in over three hundred vetoes. His unflagging industry enabled him to detect intrigue and fraud where it would have escaped the attention of a more easy-going Chief Executive; and he set his face like flint against all sharpers, big and little.

Is it merely negative to say Thou Shalt Not? Is there no affirmation in resistance to evil? Resistance can do this much: it can stop the leaks in the public treasury, and return to the people millions of acres of public lands. It can transform the Monroe Doctrine from an expression of opinion into a principle of international law. It can lift a man out of the ruck and give him an honorable name for all time. And it can refresh the spirits of citizens, and help to restore a waning faith in republics.

Public Utterances

II

The following quotations, dealing with a variety of topics, are taken from Grover Cleveland's public addresses. The reader may not, in all instances, agree with the opinions expressed; but from a perusal of these passages he can gain a definite impression of Cleveland's style of composition, his humor, his good sense, and his argumentative force.

THE NEGRO PROBLEM

(Address to Southern Educational Association, New York City, April 14, 1903.)

I believe that the days of "Uncle Tom's Cabin" are passed. I believe that neither the decree that made the slaves free, nor the enactment that suddenly invested them with the rights of citizenship any more purged them of their racial and slavery-bred imperfections and deficiencies than it changed the color of their skins.

I believe that among the nearly nine millions of negroes who have intermixed with our citizenship there is still a grievous amount of ignorance, a sad amount of viciousness and a tremendous amount of laziness and thriftlessness. I believe that these conditions inexorably present to the white people of the United States—to each in his environment and under the mandate of good citizenship—a problem, which neither enlightened self-interest nor the higher motive of human sympathy will permit them to put aside.

I believe our fellow-countrymen in the Southern and late slave-holding States, surrounded by about nine-tenths, or nearly eight millions, of this entire negro population, and who regard their material prosperity, their peace, and even the safety of their civilization, interwoven with the negro problem, are entitled to our utmost consideration and sympathetic fellowship. I am thoroughly convinced that the efforts of Booker Washington and the methods of Tuskegee Institute point the way to a safe and beneficent solution of the vexatious negro problem at the South; and I know that the good people at the North, who have aided these efforts and methods, have illustrated the highest and best citizenship and the most Christian and enlightened philanthropy.

I cannot, however, keep out of my mind tonight the thought that, with all we of the North may do, the realization of our hopes for the negro must, after all, mainly depend, except so far as it rests with the negroes themselves, upon the sentiment and conduct of the leading and responsible white men of the South, and upon the maintenance of a kindly and helpful feeling on their part toward those in their midst who so much need their aid and encouragement.

I do not know how it may be with other Northern friends of the negro, but I have faith in the honor and sincerity of the respectable white people of the South in their relations with the negro and his improvement and well being. They do not believe in the social equality of the race, and they make no false pretense in regard to it. That this does not grow out of hatred of the negro is very plain. It seems to me that there are abundant sentiment and abundant behavior among the Southern whites toward the negro to make us doubt the justice of charging this denial of social equality to prejudice, as we usually understand the word. Perhaps it is born of something so much deeper and more imperious than prejudice as to amount to a radical instinct. Whatever it is, let us remember that it had condoned the negro's share in the humiliation and spoliation of the white men of the South during the saturnalia of reconstruction days, and has allowed a kindly feeling for the negro to survive the time when the South was deluged by the perilous flood of indiscriminate, unintelligent and blighting negro suffrage. Whatever it is, let us try to be tolerant and considerate of the feelings and even the prejudice or radical instinct of our white fellow-countrymen of the South who, in the solution of the negro problem must, amid their own surroundings, bear the heat of the day and stagger under the weight of the white man's burden.

DOCTORS AND LAWYERS

(Address to the Medical Alumni Association, New York City, February 15, 1890.)

I have no doubt that it is very funny for people to caricature doctors as playing into the hands of undertakers, and to represent lawyers as being on such good terms with the evil one as to preclude the least chance of their salvation. Those who indulge in this sort of merriment are well people and people who have no lawsuits on hand. They grow very serious when their time comes and they grow sick or are caught in the meshes of the law. Then they are very respectful and very appreciative of our skill and learning. If sick they would fain have the doctor by their side day and night; and if they are troubled with a lawsuit they sit like Mordecai at the lawyer's gate and are unwilling that he should attend to any business but theirs. They are ready to lay their fortunes at our feet and to give and promise all things if they can but recover their health or win their suit. These are the days in which the lawyer, if he is wise, will suggest to his clients the payment of a round retainer or a fee in advance. I mention this as indicating a difference at this time in our situations in favor of the lawyer which gives him a slight advantage over his medical brother.

When the patient recovers, or the client has succeeded in his suit, the old hardihood and impenitence return. The patient insists that his strong constitution carried him through, and the client declares that he always knew there was nothing in the case of his adversary. They haggle over our bills and wonder how we can charge so much for so little work.

But sometimes the life or the lawsuit cannot be saved. In such a case we must not overlook a difference in our situations, with features in favor of the doctor. The defeated client is left in a vigorous and active condition, not only in the complete enjoyment of his ancient privilege of swearing at the Court, but also with full capacity to swear at his lawyer. The defeated patient, on the contrary, is very quiet indeed and can only swear at his doctor if he has left his profanity in a phonograph to be ground out by his executor.

A point of resemblance between us is found in the fact that in neither profession do we manage well in treating our own cases. Doctors solemnly advise their patients that it is dangerous to eat this or drink that, or do many other things which make existence pleasant; and after marking out a course for their poor patients which, if followed, robs life of all which makes it worth living, they hasten away to tempt instant death, according to their own teachings, by filling themselves with all the good things and indulgence within the reach of their desires. So the lawyer, safe and wise when he counsels others, deals so poorly with his own legal affairs as to have originated the saying that a lawyer who tries his own case has a fool for a client; and it seems almost impossible for a lawyer to draw his own will in such manner as not to yield a passage through it for a coach and four.

THE USES OF EX-PRESIDENTS
(Address to the New York Chamber of Commerce, November 19, 1889.)

There has been much discussion lately concerning the disposition which should be made of our ex-Presidents, and many plans have been suggested for putting us out of the way. I am sure we are very sorry to make so much trouble, but I do hope that, whatever conclusion may be reached, the recommendation of a Kentucky newspaper editor, to take us out and shoot us, will not be adopted. Prior to the 4th day of last March I did not appreciate as well as I do now the objections to this proceeding, but I have had time to reflect upon the subject since and I find excellent reasons for opposing this plan.

(Address to Neighbors, Sandwich, Mass., July 25, 1891.)

It must be admitted that our people are by no means united in their ideas concerning the place which our ex-Presidents ought to occupy, or the disposition which should be made of them. Of course, the subject would be relieved of all uncertainty and embarrassment if every President would die at the end of his term. This does not seem, however, to meet the views of those who under such an arrangement would be called on to do the dying; and so some of them continue to live, and thus perpetuate the perplexity of those who burden themselves with plans for their utilization or disposition.

A very amusing class among these anxious souls make us useful by laying upon our shoulders all sorts of political conspiracies.

If they are to be believed, we are constantly engaged in plotting for our own benefit and advancement, and are quite willing, for the sake of reaching our ends, not only to destroy the party to which we belong, but to subvert popular liberty and utterly uproot our free American institutions. Others seem of the opinion that we should be utilized as orators at county fairs and other occasions of all sorts and at all sorts of places. Some think we should interfere in every political contest, and should be constantly in readiness to express an opinion on every subject of a political character that anybody has the ingenuity to suggest. Others still regard it as simply dreadful for us to do these things, and are greatly disturbed every time an ex-President ventures to express an opinion on any subject. Not a few appear to think we should simply exist and be blind, deaf, and dumb the remainder of our days.

In the midst of all this a vast majority of the plain American people are, as usual, sound and sensible. They are self-respecting enough and have dignity enough to appreciate the fact that their respect and confidence as neighbors is something which an ex-President may well covet, and which, like any other man, he ought to earn.

THE EDUCATED MAN IN POLITICS

(Address at Harvard University, November 9, 1886.)

If the fact is recalled that only twelve of my twenty-one precedessors in office had the advantage of a collegiate or university education, a proof is presented of the democratic sense of our people, rather than an argument against the supreme value of the best and most liberal education in high public positions. There certainly can be no sufficient reason for any space or distance between the walks of a most classical education and the way that leads to a political place. Any disinclination on the part of the most learned and cultured of our citizens to mingle in public affairs, and the consequent abandonment of political activity to those who have but little regard for student and scholar in politics, are not favorable conditions under a government such as ours, and if they have existed to a damaging extent, very recent events appear to indicate that the education and conservatism of the land are to be hereafter more plainly heard in the expression of the popular will.

Surely the splendid destiny which awaits a patriotic effort in behalf of our country will be sooner reached if the best of our thinkers and educated men shall deem it a solemn duty of citizenship to engage actively and practically in political affairs, and if the force and power of their thought and learning shall be willingly or unwillingly acknowledged in party management. . . .

After all, it comes to this: The people of the United States have one and all a sacred mission to perform, and your President, not more surely than any other citizen who loves his country, must assume part of the responsibility of the demonstration to the world of the success of popular government. No man can hide his talent in a napkin, and escape the condemnation which his slothfulness deserves, or evade the stern sentence which his faithlessness invites.

ADVICE TO UNDERGRADUATES

(Address at University of Michigan, Ann Arbor, February 22, 1892.)

I beg you, therefore, to take with you, when you go forth to assume the obligations of American citizenship, as one of the best gifts of your Alma Mater, a strong and abiding faith in the value and potency of a good conscience and a pure heart. Never yield one iota to those who teach that these are weak and childish things, not needed in the struggle of manhood with the stern realities of life. Interest yourselves in public affairs as a duty of citizenship; but do not surrender your faith to those who discredit and debase politics by scoffing at sentiment and principle, and whose political activity consists in attempts to gain popular support by cunning devices and shrewd manipulation. You will find plenty of these who will smile at your profession of faith, and tell you that truth and virtue and honesty and goodness were well enough in the old days when Washington lived, but are not suited to the present size and development of our country and the progress we have made in the art of political management. Be steadfast. The strong and sturdy oak still needs the support of its native earth, and, as it grows in size and spreading branches, its roots must strike deeper in the soil which warmed and fed its first tender sprout. You will be told that the people have no longer any desire for the things you profess. Be not deceived. The people are not dead, but sleeping. They will awaken in good time, and scourge the money-changers from their sacred temple.

You may be chosen to public office. Do not shrink from it, for holding office is also a duty of citizenship. But do not leave your faith behind you. Every public office, small or great, is held in trust for your fellow-citizens. They differ in importance, in responsibility, and in the labor they impose; but the duties of none of them can be well performed if the mentorship of a good conscience and pure heart be discarded. Of course, other equipment is necessary, but without this mentorship all else is insufficient. In times of gravest responsibility it will solve your difficulties; in the most trying hour it will lead you out of perplexities, and it will, at all times, deliver you from temptation.

Correspondence

III

Some of the letters written by Grover Cleveland, particularly when the writer was moved by emotion or sentiment, have a pungency of statement and a felicity of phrasing not always present in his other compositions. Cleveland wrote many letters, at all stages of his career; but unfortunately the greater bulk of his correspondence has not so far been collected and printed. Of the letters which have been published the following are especially notable.

TO HIS BROTHER WILLIAM ON THE EVE OF HIS ELECTION AS GOVERNOR

Buffalo, N. Y., November 7, 1882.

MY DEAR BROTHER:

I have just voted. I sit here in the mayor's office alone, with the exception of an artist from Frank Leslie's newspaper, who is sketching the office. If mother was here I should be writing to her, and I feel as if it were time for me to write to someone who will believe what I write.

I have been for some time in the atmosphere of certain success, so that I have been sure that I should assume the duties of the high office for which I have been named. I have tried hard, in the light of this fact, to appreciate properly the responsibilities that will rest upon me, and they are much, too much, underestimated. But the thought that has troubled me is, can I well perform my duties, and in such a manner as to do some good to the people of the State? I know there is room for it, and I know that I am honest and sincere in my desire to do well; but the question is whether I know enough to accomplish what I desire.

The social life which seems to await me has also been a subject of much anxious thought. I have a notion that I can regulate that very much as I desire; and, if I can, I shall spend very little time in the purely ornamental part of the office. In point of fact, I will tell you, first of all others, the policy I intend to adopt, and that is, to make the matter a business engagement between the people of the State and myself, in which the obligation on my side is to perform the duties assigned me with an eye single to the interest of my employers. I shall have no idea of reelection, or any higher political preferment in my head, but be very thankful and happy if I can well serve one term as the people's Governor. Do you know that if mother were alive, I should feel so much safer? I have always thought that her prayers had much to do with my success. I shall expect you all to help me in that way.

Your affectionate brother,

Grover Cleveland.

TO A POLITICIAN WHO HAD ENDORSED A WORTHLESS OFFICE SEEKER

Executive Mansion,
Washington, August 1, 1885.

DEAR SIR:

I have read your letter with amazement and indignation. There is one—but one— mitigation to the perfidy which your letter discloses, and that is found in the fact you confess your share in it. I don't know whether you are a Democrat or not, but if you are the crime which you confess is the more unpardonable.

The idea that this administration, pledged to give the people better officers and engaged in a hand-to-hand fight with the bad elements of both parties, should be betrayed by those who ought to be worthy of implicit trust, is atrocious, and such treason to the people and to the party ought to be punished by imprisonment.

Your confession comes too late to be of immediate use to the public service, and I can only say that, while this is not the first time I have been deceived and misled by lying and treacherous representations, you are the first one that has so frankly owned his grievous fault. If any comfort is to be extracted from this assurance you are welcome to it.

Grover Cleveland.

TO MRS. HENRY WARD BEECHER ON THE DEATH OF HER HUSBAND

Executive Mansion,
Washington, D. C., May 22, 1888.

MY DEAR MRS. BEECHER:

I have been asked to furnish a contribution to a proposed memorial of your late husband.

While I am by no means certain that anything I might prepare would be worthy of a place among the eloquent and beautiful tributes which are sure to be presented, this request spurs to action my desire and intention to express to you, more fully than I have yet done, my sympathy in your affliction and my appreciation of my own and the country's loss in the death of Mr. Beecher.

More than thirty years ago I repeatedly enjoyed the opportunity of hearing him in his own pulpit. His warm utterances, and the earnest interest he displayed in the practical things related to useful living, the hopes he inspired, and the manner in which he relieved the precepts of Christianity from gloom and cheerlessness, made me feel that, though a stranger, he was my friend. Many years afterward we came to know each other; and since that time my belief in his friendship, based upon acquaintance and personal contact, has been to me a source of the greatest satisfaction.

*   *   *   *   *   *   *

Your personal affliction in his death stands alone, in its magnitude and depth. But thousands wish that their sense of loss might temper your grief, and that they, by sharing your sorrow, might lighten it.

Such kindly assurances, and your realization of the high and sacred mission accomplished in your husband's useful life, furnish all this world can supply of comfort; but your faith and piety will not fail to lead you to a higher and better source of consolation.

Yours very sincerely,

Grover Cleveland.

TO RICHARD WATSON GILDER ABOUT AN
AUTOBIOGRAPHY

Princeton, N. J., Jan. 28, 1905.

. . . I honestly think, my dear Gilder, that
there are things in my life and career that
if set out, and read by the young men of our
country, might be of benefit to a generation
soon to have in their keeping the safety and
the mission of our nation; but I am not certain of this, for I am by no means sure that
it would be in tune with the vaudeville that
attracts our people and wins their applause.
Somehow I don't want to appear wearing a
fur coat in July.

Mr. —————— and all the forces about him
have lately importuned me, in season and
out of season, to write, say, 12 autobio-
graphical articles, offering what seems to me
a large sum for them; but I have declined
the proposition. I went so far (for I soften-
ed up a bit under the suggestion of duty and
money), to inquire how something would do
like talking to another person for publica-
tion; but that did not take at all. I don't
really think I would have done even that, but
the disapproval of merely a hint that the "I"
might to an extent be eliminated, made it
seem to me more than ever, that the reten-
tion of everything that might attract the

lovers of a "snappy life" was considered important by the would-be publisher.

There is a circle of friends like you, who I hope will believe in me. I am happy in the conviction that they will continue in the faith whether an autobiography is written or not. I want my wife and children to love me now, and hereafter to proudly honor my memory. They will have my autobiography written on their hearts where every day they may turn the pages and read it. In these days what else is there that is worth while to a man nearly sixty-eight years old?

Yours faithfully,

Grover Cleveland.

("Grover Cleveland: A Record of Friendship."
By Richard Watson Gilder.)

Anecdotes and Estimates

IV

As supplementary to a chronological review of a man's career, the recital of typical episodes in his life, about affairs both important and incidental, is often valuable in helping us to round out the picture.   The anecdotes of friends, and the estimates of contemporaries, carry the flavor and color of personality.   The following quotations are drawn from various sources, and are reproduced here partly because they are interesting in themselves, and partly because they illustrate salient features of Cleveland's character.   In each case the authorship is recorded at the end of the quotation.

MCKINLEY'S ASSASSINATION

On the afternoon that President McKinley was shot at Buffalo, he was fishing with a friend in a small lake in the Berkshires.   At about sunset a man was seen rowing rapidly out towards the ex-President's boat.   "Mr. Cleveland, Mr. Cleveland," he shouted as he drew within call, "President McKinley has been assassinated!"

The ex-President did not start; he simply looked at the stranger, too much amazed by this bolt out of the blue to say anything. The man came nearer. "I tell you," he repeated, panting from his rapid rowing, "President McKinley has been shot—killed!"

Mr. Cleveland scrutinized the stranger a moment in grave silence, betraying nothing of what he thought or felt. Then making a sign to show that he had heard and appreciated what the man wished to say, his gaze dropped to his line again, though of course he was not thinking of fishing now. The bearer of bad tidings looked at the apparently stolid figure of the silent fisherman. "You don't seem to be much excited about it," he muttered, and putting about rowed slowly to shore. . . .

Later, when Mr. McKinley died, the whole world, including, no doubt, the stranger in the rowboat, was surprised and touched at the depth of feeling shown by this rugged old statesman in his public utterance concerning the Nation's great calamity.

("Mr. Cleveland: A Personal Impression." By Jesse Lynch Williams.)

BREAKING IT BLUNTLY

He spoke of a certain large city where he had appointed a good postmaster. The question was on the assistant postmaster. A tremendous effort was made to have him appoint the local Democratic boss, the kind of boss, as he believed, who represented the most venal elements in both of the great parties. They sent on a delegation consisting of the postmaster himself, and some men who were classed as the President's friends. The ex-governor of the State, also a political friend, came, and either in that or another conversation alône pressed the appointment upon him very hard. The President told him he was surprised that the ex-governor should give in to such a request; the answer was that the candidate had played so fair in the election, had done so well, that although there had been no promises, they felt it was only just to recognize his services; a good thing for the party, etc.

"When the delegation had finished speaking, I looked out of the window a while, then said: 'Gentlemen: Blank Blank will never in any circumstances be appointed assistant postmaster of Blank.' Then I looked out of the window again."

("Grover Cleveland: A Record of Friendship."
By Richard Watson Gilder.)

A SILLY ASS SEEKS A FAVOR

Cleveland was most satisfactory as president in his quick and decisive judgment upon matters presented to him. There were no delays, no revisions; in fact, no diplomatic methods of avoiding a disagreeable decision. He told you in the briefest time and in the cleverest way what he would do.

A great social leader and arbiter in social affairs in New York was very desirious that the president should reverse his judgment in regard to an appointment affecting a member of his family. I gave him a letter which procured him a personal and confidential interview. When he came back to me he said: "That is the most extraordinary man I ever saw. After he had heard me through, he said he understood the matter thoroughly and would not change his opinion or action. He has no social position and never had. I tried to present its attractions and my ability to help him in that regard, but he only laughed; yes, he positively laughed."

("My Memories of Eighty Years,"
By Chauncey M. Depew.)

THE VENEZUELAN MESSAGE

Just before its transmission—and after the final settlement of its form with the official most interested—the President began to read it to a member close to him in personal confidence as well as in direct interest. . . . . When the reading was completed, the President turned to his listener and asked: "Now, what do you think of it?" and getting the reply, "It seems to me that, towards the end, it is just a little bit tart," he said quickly, shaking his head as he always did when he wanted to put peculiar emphasis upon anything, "That is just what I intended."

("Recollections of Grover Cleveland." By George F. Parker.)

ON THE FALL RIVER BOAT

I never saw him have to repel familiarity except once. This was one evening on the deck of a Fall River boat, when a stranger broke into a group about the ex-President, with words he would not have uttered had he been in a condition to realize their impertinence. Mr. Cleveland suddenly raised his voice in a single vibrant sentence; and the episode soon came to an end.

Wherever he went there was apt to be a crowd—even when he was not President—and always a friendly one. At times on the dock at Fall River there would be a rush upon him of hundreds of people, some of whom seemed determined, at least, to touch him, when there was not time or opportunity to shake hands. He was always good-natured about it, and particularly glad to shake hands with workingmen. On the boat he would try to get to our state-rooms first, and if there was a choice, he would take possession of the least comfortable room himself, and could not be dislodged.

("Grover Cleveland: A Record of Friendship," By Richard Watson Gilder.)

FISHING WITH JOSEPH JEFFERSON

Former President Cleveland and Jefferson were great friends and frequent companions in fishing excursions. This mutual preference for the same sport ripened the intimacy between them. . . . . In their fishing jaunts there were rules implied and expressed. There was "the hour limit," for example. The boat once anchored remained so, no matter what fortune attended, for at least the space of an hour. Conversation might always be interrupted abruptly for good fishing, but under no circumstances, it is related, could good fishing be interrupted for conversation. . . . . One of a party with Cleveland and Jefferson recounts that, the preparations for departure being nearly complete, Jefferson set off on a discussion of telepathic influence. As he halted for a second, Mr. Cleveland interrupted with:

"That's all right, but where's the bait?"

Francis Wilson; Scribner's Magazine; February, 1906.)

A JOKE ON HIMSELF

Once "while in Washington," to use the ex-President's phrase for being President, he brought home a number of wild swans he had shot down South, and sent one as a compliment to each member of his Cabinet and to some of his other associates. "Well, all the boys thanked me politely for remembering them, but none of them seemed to have much to say about how they enjoyed the birds. Carlisle, I found, had his cooked on a night when he was dining out. Another, when I asked him, said he hoped I wouldn't mind, but he had sent it home to his old mother. Thurber didn't mention his bird at all for two days. Finally I asked him about it. 'Thurber, did you get that swan all right?'

" 'Yes, sir, oh, yes, I got the swan all right, thank you,' and he bent over his desk, and seemed to be very busy.

" 'Fine bird,' I said.

" 'Yes, sir, fine bird,' and went on working.

" 'Enjoy eating him, Thurber?'

"He waited a minute, then he said—'Well, sir, I guess they didn't cook him right at my house. They cooked him only two days,' and he went on working without cracking a smile."

("Mr. Cleveland: A Personal Impression."
By Jesse Lynch Williams.)

LONG PAST MIDNIGHT

It so happened once that, as I looked across the hall to the half-open door turned toward mine, I saw, reflected upon its polished surface, the hand of a man busily writing. I knew that this door opened into the workroom of Grover Cleveland, President of the United States, whom I had not seen since taking up my hard task inside his official residence. So the habit was formed, when I went early to my daily task, of asking the watchman at what hour the President had knocked off the preceding night. I found that it was generally about three o'clock in the morning; now and then, when he had finished some severe task that he had set himself, he would stop at two o'clock. My only personal knowledge, of course, was, in general, up to one o'clock. I did keep at it, once or twice, until two, in the hope that I might rival the man next door, of whose greediness for work I had heard and of which I now had abundant knowledge.

("Recollections of Grover Cleveland,"
By George F. Parker.)

TILDEN'S JIBE

This habit of personal attention to all the detailed work of his office he accomplished only by denying himself the sleep which a man of more nervous organization would have imperatively required. . . . How far this habit was due to supereminent conscientiousness, how far to temperament, it is difficult to say. Mr. Tilden evidently attributed it to temperament. "What kind of a man is this Cleveland?" he was once asked. "Oh," was the reply, in that thin, squeaky voice which characterized his later years, "he is the kind of man who would rather do something badly for himself than to have somebody else do it well."

(Outlook Magazine; December 11, 1909; on Parker's "Recollections.")

AT THE FIRST INAUGURATION

I saw Cleveland and Arthur sitting side by side in the Senate Chamber on March 4th. My first impression of Cleveland was extremely unfavorable. The contrast with Arthur, who was a fine, handsome figure, was very striking. Cleveland's coarse face, his heavy, inert body, his great, shapeless hands, confirmed in my mind the attacks made upon him during the campaign. . . . Later I came to entertain a great respect for Cleveland, to admire the courage and conscientiousness of his character.

("Autobiography." By Robert M. La Follette.)

Not long after Mr. Cleveland's marriage, being in Washington, I made a box party, embracing Mrs. Cleveland, and the Speaker and Mrs. Carlisle, at one of the theaters where Madame Modjeska was appearing. The ladies expressing a desire to meet the famous Polish actress who had so charmed them, I took them after the play behind the scenes. Thereafter we returned to the White House where supper was waiting us, the President amused and pleased, when told of the agreeable incident.

The next day there began to buzz reports to the contrary. At first covert, they gained in volume and currency until a distinguished Republican party leader put his imprint upon them in an after-dinner speech, going the length of saying the newly-wedded Chief Magistrate had actually struck his wife and forbidden me the Executive Mansion, though I had been there every day during the week that followed.

Mr. Cleveland believed the matter too preposterous to be given any credence and took it rather stoically. But naturally Mrs. Cleveland was shocked and outraged, and I made haste to stigmatize it as a lie out of whole cloth. Yet though this was sent away

by the Associated Press and published broadcast I have occasionally seen it referred to
by persons over eager to assail a man in-
capable of an act of rudeness to a woman.

("Marse Henry, an Autobiography."
By Henry Watterson.)

A YOUNG VISITOR

One day early in the summer, while sitting on the recessed piazza overlooking Sip-
pican Harbor, Mr. Cleveland was visited by
a small youngster, unattended, who wished
to pay his respects, with due formality, and
assure the newcomer that he was very welcome to Marion. Mr. Cleveland greeted the
polite lad as solemnly as the importance of
the occasion demanded. In the course of the
interchange of courtesies, it became evident
that the visitor was under a misapprehen-
sion, for when Mr. Cleveland referred to
the fact that he had been defeated in the
late election, and declared that the people did
not want him in the White House any longer,
the boy exclaimed: "Oh, I had not heard of
that, Sir!" and expressed the greatest sympathy at the untoward event.

I saw no betrayal of inward amusement
on Mr. Cleveland's face. All went as grave-
ly as if the colloquy had taken place in the
Blue Room between the Chief Executive and
a foreign ambassador.

("Grover Cleveland: A Record of Friendship."
By Richard Watson Gilder.)

BABY RUTH RECITES

Ruth, the eldest, was then about three years old. There was a joyful Christmas at the White House, and General John M. Wilson, who during both administrations was Mr. Cleveland's aide, describes an incident of the day as the most touching he ever witnessed—Ruth, in holiday attire, under a beautiful Christmas tree, repeating the Psalm beginning, "The Lord is my shepherd," and at its conclusion Mr. Cleveland taking the child up into his strong arms and kissing her, while tears were raining down his cheeks.

(Anecdotes of President Cleveland; Century Magazine; March, 1913.)

HOW IT FEELS TO BE PRESIDENT

"A sensitive man is not happy as President," he said. "It is fight, fight, fight, all the time. . . . I looked forward to the close of my term as a happy release from care. But I am not sure that I wasn't more unhappy out of office than in. A term in the presidency accustoms a man to great duties. He gets used to handling tremendous enterprises, to organizing forces that may affect at once and directly the welfare of the world. After the long exercise of power, the ordinary affairs of life seem petty

[91]

and commonplace. An ex-President practicing law or going into business is like a locomotive hauling a delivery wagon. He has lost his sense of proportion. The concerns of other people and even his own affairs seem too small to be worth bothering about. I thought I was glad when Mr. McKinley came to Washington to be inaugurated, and I took a drink of rye whiskey with him in the White House and shook hands with him and put my hat on my head and walked out a private citizen. But I miss the strain, the spur to constant thinking, the consciousness of power, the knowledge that I was acting for seventy million people daily."

(In The Interpreter's House; American
Magazine; September, 1908.)

THE OPINIONS OF FOUR REPUBLICANS

"The fame of Grover Cleveland is secure because of the ruggedness, the simplicity of his character, and because of his inflexible determination in executing his honest judgment."

Charles Evans Hughes.

"Grover Cleveland earned the sincere gratitude of his countrymen. . . . He was a great President. . . . Throughout his political life he showed those rugged virtues of the public servant and citizen, the emulation of which by those who follow him will render progress of our political life toward better things a certainty."

William Howard Taft.

"The powerful influence of a strong and noble character made manifest in high station is the chief legacy of Grover Cleveland to his countrymen. . . . With high and unquestioning courage he stood always for what he believed to be just and honest and best for his country. With unconcealed scorn and wrath he stood against all sham and chicanery."

Elihu Root.

"As mayor of the city, as governor of his state, and twice as President, he showed signal powers as an administrator, coupled with entire devotion to the country's good, and a courage that quailed before no hostility when once he was convinced where his duty lay."

Theodore Roosevelt.

BIBLIOGRAPHY

V

No standard or comprehensive life of Grover Cleveland has yet appeared. The best books to read are the following.

On Cleveland:
"Recollections of Grover Cleveland."
By George F. Parker.

"Grover Cleveland: A Record of Friendship."
Ry Richard Watson Gilder.

"Mr. Cleveland: A Personal Impression."
By Jesse Lynch Williams.

By Cleveland:
"Addresses, State Papers and Letters."
"Presidential Problems."
"Fishing and Shooting Sketches."

On the History of the Period:
"Twenty Years of the Republic, 1885-1905."
By Harry Thurston Peck.

CPSIA information can be obtained
at www.ICGtesting.com
Printed in the USA
BVHW032032050519
547421BV00001B/107/P